Praise for

TASTE MY WORDS

"Poems in *Taste My Words* offer up an eclectic menu in a delightful rendering of the human condition seen through a keen poetic eye, delving into existential questions of who we are to others and most importantly, to ourselves." —Ray Williams' is a writer of short stories and poems. His work appeared in the Pakaraima Anthology *Scaling New Heights*.

"Lisa Freemantle's poems dives into personal and riveting universal themes, provoking nostalgia into one's own journey. A must read for lovers of poetic beauty!" —Habeeb Alli, Co-Author of *Scaling Heights 2022* and President of Pakaraima Writers Association

"With her poems that warm the heart and cleanse the soul, Lisa Freemantle never fails to enchant and capture the imagination." —Ken Puddicombe, author, *Unfathomable and Other Poems*

"Taste My Words is a joyful triumph. Freemantle's compositions are imbued with a highly poetic energy instilling in the reader a subtle, penetrating fever of contentment... Such engaging imagery conceptualizes youth, death and life; nature's subtle rule over all that lives." —Dr. Franklin Mohan, author *Love Has Two Moons and Other Stories*

ALSO BY
LISA FREEMANTLE

Co-Author: Words for the Journey Series

Words for the Journey

Words for the Journey for Kids

Words for the Journey for Teens

Poems in the Anthology

Scaling New Heights

TASTE MY WORDS

Poems

Lisa Freemantle

www.middleroadpublishers.ca

Making Literature See The Light Of Day

Library and Archives Canada Cataloguing in Publication

ISBN 978-1-990765-06-3 (softcover)

Front Cover photograph courtesy of

Adonyi Gabor and Pexels.com

Cover Design by Ken Puddicombe and Kathryn Lagerquist

TASTE MY WORDS
POEMS
Lisa Freemantle

"I do not sleep to dream but dream to change the world."

Martin Carter (1927-1997)

DEDICATION

To my Uncle Lester Fernandes, who has always believed in my creativity and encouraged me to share my work, to my supportive husband Jim and to my wonderfully creative children, Valerie, Alexander and Benjamin, to my mother Berl who first fostered my writing, and finally to my dear siblings, cousins and good friends who all read, listen to and appreciate my offerings.

I love you all.

ACKNOWLEDGMENTS

To my family: Jim, Valerie, Alex and Ben, thank you all so much for being my sounding boards for new poems, for being there on good and bad days and for letting me unknowingly bounce off you all, my endless snippets of ideas.

To my sisters Kim and Rehannah and my cousins Christine and Linda: I really appreciated you all reading my creations and giving me your candid feedback. Your combined enthusiasm for my work fueled my creativity.

To my Uncle Lester Fernandes: Thank you for always taking your time in responding, mulling over, or as you called it 'taking time digesting' each of my pieces, each word, each phrase and then when you were ready, giving me your measured honest opinion on what insights found within. It has meant the world to me that you really 'saw' what I was trying to say, appreciated my efforts and on occasion found my poems 'brilliant'. Thank you too for always encouraging me to not only continue writing and but also to continue sharing my poetry with others.

Finally, my grateful thanks go to my editor Kenneth Puddicombe for his patience, his careful reading of my poetry and his thoughtful comments throughout. I have been truly blessed.

Table of Contents

INTRODUCTION

I have been writing poetry all my life.

I love the 'taste' of words—how they go together, how they sound, how they feel and how they evoke emotions in myself and others. I write because writing completes me, makes me feel whole, balanced and content. I write to better articulate and understand the world around me.

Even though I pour my heart and soul into every work I compose, most of my poetry is not strictly autobiographical. I write about the human condition: things I may have experienced, or personally witnessed but more often than not, I write about what I 'see' looking through the windows of others. I also write about the natural world. There is just so much scope out there.

My poems are like my children—good or bad—whether they convey the messages I intend or not, whether they are understood, whether people like them or not, I love them all the same.

I invite you to *Taste my Words* and I hope that you will find some delicious morsels here to satisfy your creative appetite.

Lisa Freemantle

TASTE MY WORDS

Some of my words are spicy and hot
Others are bland, but most are not
Nibble and tongue each pledge, each text
Your palate knows not what flavour is next

Will it be magic or informative reports?
Or just back and forth utterances of all sorts?
Or declaration of love or frothy remark?
Or thoughts of hate or views both light and dark?

Still… take a big bite, digest and then chew;
Pungent senses explode, exposed for clearer view.
Tangy, salt, sour and bittersweet,
Implications change with every perceptive,
prospective glance meet

For though meanings are murky
And transform each hour, each day,
Taste my words, won't you?
Let their flavour show the way

WE ARE WE POETRY INTRODUCTION

The first group of poems in this collection, I have called *We are We*. These poems speak of the common human experience, shared and understood by all mortals who live on this planet. The first selection by the same name, epitomizes this concept.

01 WE ARE WE

2nd April 2022

We are we

We exist in infinite variety
shaped by our world, our society

Molded by our choices
and shaped by the hands of others,
we are mirrored fragments,
facets of our fathers and mothers

There are no prescriptive measures,
or rigid doctrine we must rehearse;
no, our shared human mandate
is simply just living in this universe

We are we

Call us: he, she, they, me
as we grow continuously
we run in our mortal race;
each progressing at our own pace

Some of us push ourselves
to climb ever higher;
must be stronger, go longer,
keep striving, inspire

Others though, sit back
sedate, relaxed, calm;
reserved, just observe
with unruffled aplomb

But whatever we be:
driven or free
we share the same innate plan,
the inner sense;

that we understand,
the true essence
we see
our naked humanity
for

We are we

02 TAPESTRY

11th February 2021

History stretches forward in time,
touches us on the shoulder and seeps into our skin

We are build-ed chronicles, molded sagas;
preordained re-occurring themes,
rooted from deep within

Though our life journeys are individual,
they are in themselves not unique
Recessed thoughts percolate;
their effects indirect, oblique

For we are a tapestry of long agos,
here and nows and tomorrows;
woven threads of past joys,
present stresses and future sorrows

Who we were, who we are
and who we will be
are all one in the same, actually
They are transected yet connected,
infected with one another;
we are inexorably linked
to our inner father, mother, sister, brother

The bonds are inescapable,
no matter where we turn,

they pull and push
and these entwining strands yearn
to fabricate, cultivate
and create a new telling of our joined story:
past history, future memory compelling
It is an eternally winding and meandering life tale
fed fresh by our present-day trivial detail

So...ensure your knitted fibres remain
moral, just and strong

for it is to future generations

that they will evermore belong

03 LEND MY PEN

24th January 2021

Lend my pen to your eyes;
Eyes open to observe, explore, view
and with discerning perception, bear witness to
entire life tomes, every chapter, every page
articulated, beautifully written about at every stage;
No myopic vision, do not limit your sight;
Do not stay in the darkness, come into the light
Young, new, old and wise,
please, lend my pen to your eyes

Lend my eyes to your mind;
Mind open to ponder what is seen
and gain understanding of what authentic living means
Every facet, every aspect, every idea, every plan,
be you child, adolescent, woman or man;
Do not limit your awareness or attitude
or accept the random platitude;
Consider, contemplate all you find;
Please, lend my eyes to your mind

Lend my mind to your mouth;
Mouth open to express inner ideas and notions,
every true belief, every genuine emotion;
Be fluent in articulating all manner of thought
Communicate! Some may agree with you…or not
Do not suffer to be silent, speak, speak aloud!

Let your opinions be known, be confident, be proud
Voice your observations to east, west, north and south,
Please, lend my mind to your mouth

Lend my mouth to your ears;
Ears open to actively attend and take heed
to every word others say, for their truth kernels, their seed;
For much can be learned when you stop and take note:
knowledge, shared confidences or sweet anecdote
Do not block out voices or ignore the sound,
for wisdom is gained to one listening all around
Be truly there for the triumphs, be there for the tears,
Please, lend my mouth to your ears

Lend my ears to your hands;
Hands open to applaud what has been heard;
Make every act, every manipulation, the “word” transferred.
Wave, squeeze, hug, shake, handle and hold;
True faith, true love, true peace; are all gold!
Do not avoid the chance to put a smile on a face
for welcomes are garnered in every embrace;
Let your contributions be felt throughout all lands;
Please, lend my ears to your hands

Lend my hands to your feet;
Feet open to walk to hand-wrought change
with every step, every stride, extend your range;
Move to souls disenfranchised, poor, alone;
Tread in the obscure shoes of little renown
Do not saunter past those who have need of your aid;
Help them to not be lost, friendless or afraid.
Yes climb, run, amble, hike to all you would meet;
Please, lend my hands to your feet

Lend my feet to your pen;
Be open, not for honour or award
But for history, to teach others, share and record
Your experiences, awareness and expertise
acumen, insight, opportunities seized;
Lend my feet to your pen, eyes, mind, mouth, ears, hands, feet;
Actively seek your potential so you'll be complete
for it is in the attempt that you truly grow
and life's real treasures you'll come to know

Young, new, old and wise,
Please, lend my pen to your eyes

04 THAT WE COULD BE NEWBORN

6th January 2021

That we could be newborn;
No brush strokes of bias or scorn
but colour-blinded
not narrow-minded.

That we could live newborn;
No bigotry or misinformation,
instead a lack of intolerant discrimination
Without partiality and prejudgment forced in steps before you walk
Without unfair and prejudicial words put in mouths before you talk

That we could feel newborn
Bask in the warmth of the sun, pure clean light.
Know that all agree on what's wrong and right.
Untouched by slanted and swayed deceptions;
Our slates wiped free of any marks of preconceptions

That we could sense newborn
Envision all minds uncluttered by ego, spoil and greed,
Shared resources for everyone, nobody in need.
Our canvasses clear
Our lives lived without fear

That we could be reborn…

…to a world of innocence and acceptance by all
Where differences celebrate and stand up tall
Where welcomes are friendly and never cold
Where wars find no purchase, evils no grip to hold
Where hope lives for a brighter world view
Where ingenuity is unfettered and love is too

That we could be newborn

05 THE WORLD WEEPS

16th March 2022

The World weeps

Her shoulders shake, quake in grief
peace un-joined purloined by a thief
as a tear from her sad gaze seeps

The World bleeds

Her skin attacked, cracked and broken
thinly veils inner war still unspoken
trifling bandage not what globe needs

The World mourns

Her dear children's lives in tatters
corrupt heads decide what matters
death follows, she worries, she warns

The World waits

She yearns for soothing of sorrows
and longs for tranquil tomorrows
filled with abundant loves and not hates

For the time has come for action;
the era for decisive change.
let us pacify discordant factions;

set destruction and pain out of range

For compassion between global brothers
with open and honest exchange
will allow us to walk with each other;
make a world where division is strange

Wake up!

for Peace sleeps
hence today…

The World weeps

06 CITIZEN OF THE WORLD

16th February 2021

I am a citizen of the world.
I live, I breathe...I am.

My language might not be the same as yours,
nor the colour of my skin.
The culture I celebrate, the food I consume,
the customs I practice, may differ.
My likes and dislikes, my ... 'importances' and trivialities
may not be the same as yours.
My education, my attire and level of sophistication
may not match yours either,
And you may oppose my beliefs, my views and my opinions.

But...
Of my citizenship, my right to **be** and right to be here,
there is no question.
My very existence is my passport, my visa, my permit;
It identifies my belonging to this universe of unsettled settlers.

And so, you and I, **we** are citizens here together;
Different yes but fundamentally the same.

We the species permanently co-inhabit
the same plane of existence.
We the people suck on the same teat of Mother Earth
for nourishment.
We the human race grow, then reach our senescence
on the same planet.
We the beings live off of the same resources,
the same land, the same waters.
And breathe the same air.
Our bodies and minds all feel: love, hate, joy, sadness,
fear, assurance, hunger, thirst.

Our souls are alive.

So yes, we are different in the tiny minutia,
the inconsequential workings;
But we have *infinitely* more in common
Let's celebrate that fact.

For **we** are citizens of the world.

07 ISOLATION: HAPPY ALONE

30TH July 2020

inclusive isolation:
mind, sense formation

introspection
freedom from self-consciousness
a self-gift

space to grow creatively
merged rather than split mental energies:
a personal lift

sequestered, yet not lonely
remote yet only

set apart

one beating heart
can be recharged
empathy and intellectual clarity enlarged

so alone but not detached
concepts opened, unlatched

a focused affirmation

inclusive isolation

08 QUARANTINE

The Oher Side of Loneliness
30th July 2020

constrictive quarantine:
loneliest ever been

sequestered
cut off from all
lack of community

too much space in the between
absence of togetherness
a need for unity

pacing the halls
climbing the walls

alone

impersonal connections by phone
deserted, solo, solitary
secluded, not feeling ordinary

remote minds mismatched
idea and thoughts detached

unfocused unseen

constrictive quarantine

09 IDIOSYNCRASIES OF LIFE

1st January 2022

Life is inconsistent logic;
opposing yet equally valid points of view.

These numerous paradoxes,
shifting and fickle
though indeed contradictory,
are all true.

There are no true miracles
without real sin

And no inner beauty
without accepting the ugliness within.

One cannot deeply love
without understanding hate.

One cannot learn patience
without a long time in wait.

There is no glorious sunshine
without first, dreary rain.

One cannot truly appreciate comfort
without recognizing pain.

One cannot sincerely rejoice
without genuinely knowing sorrow.

And cannot openly lend
without learning to borrow.

Energy from lethargy
Stability from changed
Richness from poverty
Friend from estranged

Kindness from cruelty
Charity from greed
Contentment from sadness
Plenty from need

This give and take existence
conflicting harmonious appeal;
Unsettling, yet comforting;
Mercurial, enduring
...real

10 THREE DAYS

3rd April 2021

today speaks to tomorrow of yesterday.

yesterday wished today wouldn't come.

tomorrow will dream of hopes, yet blame hindsight.

today understands the now-present,
the current boons in time;
yet recognizes there was once offerings of
before and long ago
and now asks,
'what gifts will come?'

but verity,
only **now** is genuine!

murky time,
coloured history in soft rose,
indistinctly hued future unknown,
while stained in today's life-flushed dyes.

And so today-now
dreams of yet to come;
but still remembers promises unfulfilled.

yesterday was…
fleeting,
misty memory,
soft edged,
    clouded dew.

today is…
dragging,
lumpy jagged,
flawed imperfection,
achy, tired.

tomorrow will…
be dreaded?
be hopeful?
be better?

never arrive.

revolution imminent?

three days holding hands in my mind.

11 POETRY

15th June 2020

Poetry translates the mundane of everyday life
into expressive beauty

Poetry translates the mundane of life into
expressive beauty

Poetry translates the mundane of life into beauty

Poetry translates mundane of life into beauty

Poetry translates mundane life into beauty

Poetry translates life into beauty

Poetry translates into beauty

Poetry translates beauty

Poetry translates

Poetry

12 ELUSIVE DREAMS

25th August 2020

Slumber, let go, unwind
Projected images from the mind
No line ups, no wait
No ticket needed for any date
The seat, always free
Attendance is meant to be
No need to dress the part
Sit back, wait for the show to start

Each evening's fare entails
Varied genres or categories
Though similar themes may prevail
Every night, there's different stories…

Sometimes, from the audience,
you merely observe and view;
Other times, play a role,
though often a 'different' you;
Supporting cast, featured character or lead
All constraints of familiar self-image freed

Slip in and out of each visualization,
no reason or rhyme,
For just a few moments or
…for a longer time

In the moments of fantasy there is perfect clarity;
No notice taken of waking logic disparity.
Narratives disjointed, frequently make little sense;
Weaving through past, present and future tense

What do these visions mean,
whose origins are often unseen?

The unconscious mind is master;
it is free from everyday stress;
no deadlines to meet, no buttons to press,
no constraints, limitations, no restrictions or
controls.

This inner psyche directs all the action
and is not bound by outer goals.
It makes its own sense of the world,
of living, of being
and existing unrestrained,
this exercise is freeing

The brain discovers, explores crafting its own
explanations
and these nightly dreams are the results of its
creations

Plots within plots, crisscrossing overlapping,
understandable design to the souls napping

...When awareness returns,
    memory discerns faint echoes
which remain
from the dream domain

The fleeting nature of elusive reveries becomes clear
Their substance, key elements at times disappear
Like intangible wisps, images may be...
less crisp

Yet while many vanish with the dawn

...others ...linger...on.

13 SERENDIPITY I

16th June 2020

It is fortunate in life if one can:

View the world through the innocent eyes of a child
Be secure and calm in the mundane, meek and mild
Perform all daily tasks fastidiously, neatly, routinely
Indulge in all new pastimes, readily, gladly, keenly
Experience the rare, exceptional moments of grace
Discover, revel, appreciate an extraordinary place
Preserve optimism, positivity, real faith and hope
Assist one who has melancholy to better cope
Resolve to honestly attempt to do one's best
Take good care and do take sufficient rest
Readily assist a poor, needy neighbour
Thrive in clean and honest labour
Stand up for a very good cause
Humbly recognize applause
Endure a life without fear
Cheerfully do volunteer
Emote then react, feel
Share a hearty meal
Remain ever near
Be of glad cheer
Know to pass
Display class
Be free
See

14 SERENDIPITY II

16th June 2020

It is truly a privilege if one can:

Enjoy creative art and harmony and dance and song
Laugh and spread the joy of being alive all day long
Relish and enjoy changing or fluctuating weather
Be happy with exceptional, quality time together
Exchange confidences with true, trusted friends
Keep some extra coins one can share or spend
Make sure war and hatred all decisively cease
Discover world humanity ultimately at peace
Remember a special one to think highly of
Receive, impart heartfelt, abundant love
Trust in a collective honour and good
Be kind and generous as one should
Strive to do the best that you can
Toil according to the wider plan
Answer one's colleague's call
Look, perceive the best in all
Clearly do communicate
Endeavour to educate
Learn something new
Take a wider view
Please smile
Stay awhile
Agree
Be

15 BASE AND *BASE*

14th June 2020

BASE:
Love life: solid ground, all around
Foundation of intermingled human attachments
supported on bricked edifices in immoveable catchments;

Constant growth in breadth and length
yet cemented with emotional strength

BASE:
Just exist: shaky floor, nothing more
Lowest dissolution of weak human attachment;
Crumbling emotions, total detachment

Disconnections of regretful sorrow
Fade today, gone tomorrow

BASE
Secure makes for happy folks

BASE
Spineless is the cruel hoax

Which world do you live in?

16 DARE TO DREAM

27th June 2020

dare to dream in colour,
every hue, me and you

all the world's tints united, blending, shine
each belov-ed, hers, his, yours, mine

every glorious mixture: separate or fused
happy, contented, joyful, amused

no clashing, all matching
in favour, in style
then marvel the beauty
the splendour worthwhile

what a wonder
what a goal
set grief asunder
make every body whole

make it elementary
complimentary

live it, conceive it
love it, believe it

dare
to
dream
in colour

17 JUST BREATHE

26th August 2021

Life:
Ostensibly a series of repeated breaths
a regular cadence
measured beats

in…out…

in…out…

in...out…

over and over again
perpetual repeats

But these in- and ex-halations
are not identical

Twixt each pulse is new living,
a new "authentic–al"

Where reality is the speciality,
each instant different, discrete;
every spiral, twist, fold and turn
for notice does compete

It is appealing, this endless variety,
this constant moving change,

revealing all life's experiences
between each breath's wide range

For in the end,
these moments cause one

to smile or smirk,

scream or sigh,

sleep or stir,

spur on or shy,

But whatever life brings,

soothe or seethe

remember

to just

...breathe

18 MIRED INNER VISION: WORLD PANDEMIC

25th April 2021

Mired inner vision,
muddled and obscure
Riddled doubts, questions, indecision;
Future calm? murky, unsure

Media communications and disclosures,
infiltrate, permeate minds over and over again.
Miasmas of facts, figures and fictions
penetrate, oversaturate the overloaded brain.

For the world has run amok,
Though in many ways now stuck;

Ever in motion, yet standing still

So begs the notion,
a lack of ingenuity, strength or will?

Was this a preventable calamity;
this now masked insanity?

Or was it just plain bad luck?

HEART TOUCHED POEMS

The next group of poems are *Heart Touched*. These deal with various sensitive and moving life experiences: some happy: like being in love or celebrating friendship, some heartrending: like witnessing dementia in loved ones or not being able to take back something you said. Other topics in this group are disturbing, including child rape and wife abuse. Although the reader (or myself) may not have personally encountered every experience described, these poems try to empathize and understand their impact.

19 HATRED CAME IN THE NIGHT

10th July 2020

Hatred came in the night

Salty with sweat
Brutal in deed
Wicked with intent
Evil hunger to feed

Fingers of fear creeping
Expectant one, afraid, not sleeping

Then silent pain, an inner scream, inaudible, no sound
Agony arose when Hatred would pound
Eyes on blue walls all around the room
White curtains of innocence shone amidst the gloom

Paper-thin tender veneer signaled the close
Then a rezipping and realigning of clothes

Left behind, crimson stains darkening by morn
Small weeping form; quiet, forlorn
And a lingering sting and the stench of recall
Remember, stay good, you mustn't tell all

Time for rest now
A slight dulling of pain
Sigh… a short, blessed respite…

Until Hatred comes again

20 BEHIND THE EYES

11th March 2021

Golden home, diamond rings
Surrounding rich and lavish things

Posh calm outer face
Not a hair out of place
Yet look closely
Cheek tear-tracks you can trace

A plush cell, heavily padded
No one hears the inner screams
Behind heavily guarded walls
No escape e'en in her dreams

Always crying though trying to chase the pain away
Horrifying, occupying, her ache is here to stay

But what goes on behind the eyes
Buried darkness resides
Filled with untruths and lies
Hidden daily

Outward calm and complacent
Inside angry impatient
All veiled behind the eyes

Fun-filled jokes, witty charm

Lovely looking on his arm

From moment of waking
Perfect home she's making
Yet look closely
See the joy that she's faking

Self-imposed this lifetime sentence
Warden's thrown the keys away
No escaping her prison
Here it's destined she'll stay

For not today, yesterday or tomorrow will it end
No parole and no control, her life of sad pretend

But what goes on behind the eyes
There a darkness resides
Filled with untruths and lies
Hidden daily

Outward happy contentment
Inside painful resentment
All veiled behind the eyes

All veiled far behind...the eyes

21 YOU DON'T KNOW ME

19th June 2020

You don't see the real me
You praise the outer attire
The top but not inner fire

No, you don't really see the real me

You don't understand the real me,
You know the basic intent
The skin, not what's truly meant

No, you don't understand the real me

You don't really love the real me
My foibles and blunders
The overs but not the unders

No, you don't really love the real me

You don't really hear the real me
You get the words and the syntax
The surface but not the deep facts

No, you don't really hear the real me

No, you don't really know the real me

22 ONE WORD

8th June 2020

You speak
I hear

In my mind, in my ear

My heart beats its way out of my chest wall;
surely it will break

Skin flushed like scarlet cardinal's sin;
Ohhh, the body ache!

Trembling limbs lack support.
Dampness exudes no comfort.

Eyes a wonder as they gaze;
Lips are parted all amaze

Breathless am I…

Now you know why.

23 LOVE IS...

28th March 2022

Love is…

forever and firm
reflection within reflection
warm hues
endless sky

Love is…

complex yet unassuming
clarity amidst life's indistinctness
safe solace
home

Love is…

all in
all shades
all directions
always

24 DO YOU SMILE?

27th June 2020

Do you smile when I tell you I miss you
Do you smile when I tell you I'm found
Do you smile when I tell you I love you
It's been awhile, tell me, do you smile

Do you frown when I tell you I'm empty
Do you frown when I tell you it's dark
Do you frown when I tell you I worry
When I'm down, tell me, do you frown

Do you laugh when I tell you I'm funny
Do you laugh when I tell you a joke
Do you laugh when I tell you I'm witty
I'm a gaffe, tell me, do you laugh

Do you cry when I tell you I'm leaving
Do you cry when I tell you I'm sad
Do you cry when I tell you I'm lonely
Wipe my eye, tell me, do you cry

Do you pray when I tell you I'm broken
Do you pray when I tell you I'm lost
Do you pray when I tell you I'm soulless
I wish you'd say, tell me, do you pray

Do you hope when I tell you I'm changing
Do you hope when I tell you I've grown
Do you hope when I tell you I'm strengthening
An uphill slope, but tell me, do you hope

Do you sleep when I tell you I'm weary
Do you sleep when I tell you I'm bushed
Do you sleep when I tell you I'm worn out
Shallow or deep, tell me, do you sleep

Do you sigh when I tell you I'm beaten
Do you sigh when I tell you I'm spent
Do you sigh when I tell you I need you
When I fail but try, tell me, do you sigh

Smile or frown, laugh or cry
Pray or hope, sleep or sigh
Please do comply
Send your reply

25 I DON'T LIKE MIRRORS

26th May 2020

I don't like mirrors

Reflect the *you* others see,
the laughs, the show, the shell,
...the sell.

Not the you inside of me;

Not the me inside of you;

Not the feeling of the heart;

Exploiting truth.

26 SAY THE WORD, I SHALL BE HEALED

24th February 2001

There are times when I look into the mirror, O Lord,
And I do not like the person that I see.
It's incredible that you love me still despite my faults.
Although I sin you keep forgiving me.
I am not worthy to receive you, say the word I shall be healed.
You keep on forgiving me.

You have given me your blood and your body.
You have suffered so that sinners can go free.
You give your life into my hands today.
Now I know I'll live eternally.
I am not worthy to receive you, say the word I shall be healed.
Now I'll live eternally.

When I turn my back away from you in anger, O Lord;
I've discovered that you love me just the same.
For when I stop to take a moment just to listen close,
I can clearly hear you call my name.
I am not worthy to receive you, say the word I shall be healed.
I can hear you call my name.

You have given me your blood and your body.
You have washed away my sins and all my shame.
You give your life into my hands today.
Sinners are the reason why you came.
I am not worthy to receive you, say the word I shall be healed.
Sinners are just why you came.

I'm the reason why you came.
I can hear you call my name.
Now I'll live eternally...
You keep on forgiving me.

27 WINDOWS AND DOORS: (LOVERS TO FRIENDS)

13th June 2020

i can't see anything but tears.

door is closed, slammed shut, locked tight
no longer wanted, heart haunted
pain discover, not lover
no sleep, just weep tonight

locks changed; key tossed away
a new resider, fresh presider
in Your heart's home, freely She roams
and She's there to stay

but there's a window; You voice
"we can be friends, and let us mend,
come through won't you
as a good pal, you shall find it's your choice"

though the casement lies ajar
for me to visit inside
You bid me, and kid me
it's so high, i know why it's not open very wide

so heavy and sad i cannot climb
and fear sneaking sin, peeking in,
lest i view, Her and You, in private time

though alarm is silent
dare not approach the door, for it's there
i fear it, can hear it, feel it clanging loudly in my ear

So…the invite will unanswered remain
the door i can't enter nor through the window...
pain.

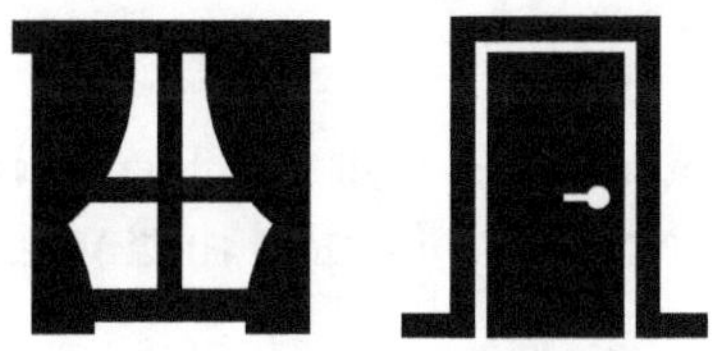

28 NO RETURN TO INNOCENCE

12th March 2022

Innocence:
    the gap between you and me
        that fissure filled with mystery

Innocence:
    the unknown oft small hidden truth
        the privacies of aged and youth

Innocence:
    emotion space where *you* are *you*
        and where *me* is honestly *me* too

No one should intrude in this personal place
No one should know all in this sacred space

For within the crevice
    individual quiet
        identities reside

For within the deep
    should be no one else
        living there inside

To know other within, unequivocally
every thought, every intimacy, every feeling
leaves no true self, no singleness,
no stone unturned, no concealing

No oneness, no distinct *you*, no separate *me*
No space between means there is only...***we***

This ***we***, this '***you-me***' is convoluted, polluted
It is boundaries smudged, pre-judged, it is ***we***,
diluted
Intertwined like one-mind
No wonders are withheld
We-notions now conceived, believed
We-thought ideas compelled

No...there is no return to innocence
to clean slate of before

No going back to not knowing
Opened knowledge, minds can't ignore

Though unspoken, pure self is broken
Forever tainted true
For memory stains and still remains
Recollection sticks like glue

So, uphold your guard,
    though it be hard
        keep heart gap round you clear

Innocence:
    our secret selves
        keeps each own enigma near

Innocence:
your private space where *you* are sincerely *you*

Innocence:
my sacred place where *me* is *myself* true

29 HEALING-PAIN-RECEDES

11th August 2020

Restoring balance hurts
For healing is pain

Reliving darkness-es long hidden again

Uproot ancient evils, now revealed
Resurfaced; they'd long been concealed
Flesh torn as each sin viewed
Foul and hated meanings construed

Minds negatively impacted
As jagged memories are extracted
The cuts, so deep
The toll paid, steep

...Time....ticks....slowly...

And... gradually, so gradually... pain recedes
Finally, look forward to see where recovery leads

And eventually, what was once previous disgraced
Becomes mended with new untainted notions replaced

And when all is said and done, some scars do remain
But no longer now bowed in shame

Stand tall, head high
Open gaze, clear-eyed
Be proud, to have survived
To have lived, grown, thrived

Evil will not win
Iniquity cannot stay
Washed clean, authentic renewal
Breathe in to a new fresh day

The balance is definitely needed
Healing is pain receded

30 THE GARDEN OF OBLIVION

For my mother
7th July 2021

her life estate, once the envy of all
now lies covered in mossy gossamer lace.
ago, her plantings were strong, abundant, tall,
now memories bequeath soft traces on her face

muted brilliance,
gentle shine;
deep time-proven roots
resilient, though now slender and fine.

unpolished sophistication falls in gentle folds around
where no sharp edges remain,
only soft green fronds abound

yet ...
rare single moments of radiance,
though subtle and hushed
break through the misted web,
brightly glowing; these cannot be crushed;
vibrant blooming remnants,
brief flashes in eyes play;

...then too soon again drops the curtain-filamented overlay.

content in her garden of oblivion,
she never complains
delicate, trusting and tender,
for it is here for her,
love remains.

31 TUNNEL VISION

(THE DARKROOM OF DEPRESSION)
17th December 2021

underground
bricked in, airless;

no hope, no light, no life,
no escape,
...prayer-less

no back or forward, no compass to point the way,
no windows or views left, right, night or day,
no street sign or speed limit, no distance marker…
just endless,
thick blackness,
bleaker, starker

mind wearied, defeated, energy sapped

why?

brain queried, depleted, hopelessly trapped

sigh…

must keep striving,
for surviving hinges on effort applied;
need to keep prodding, plodding;

for life promises hope justified.

need try to see that there will be
in time, an end to the gloom;
work hard, lower the guard,
clear doubts developed in this darkroom.

so, though passageway seems eternal,
must believe
relief will eventually come,
despair will ultimately leave

tho' still underground
glimpse fissured cracks
and burgeoning fairness;

ah…faint hope,
faint light,
faint life,

yes,
plan escape toward

…dawning new awareness

32 OLD AND NEW FRIENDS

New Year's Day, January 1, 2021

Weed away the negative
Fertilize with love
Water strengthening roots
Look to the light above

Old friends...
Mature growth withstands
all measure of bad weather;
for the established arb knows
how life's challenges and gifts work together
So, though storms, gales, blizzards,
downpours and thunder
may cause a little ruffling or bending,
over and under,
the deeply rooted form beneath
remains unchanged, always strong
because it understands it's place in life
and grasps where it belongs

Time invested in this old tree
cannot and should not be dismissed;
It's continued growth and health paramount,
for it has been sun kissed

New friends...
Now, the new wistful sapling
weaves back and forth with the gentlest breeze;

As yet unsure of its station,
the plantlet can become uprooted... with ease.
So, it uses a shield of novelty
to screen it from the daily winds of change.
This may curb some growth or extend it
in other ways, quite strange.
The exact nature of future bonded limbs,
time will of course discover;
For small slights, bumps, hurts heal rapidly;
the seedling can quickly recover

But new sprouts should not be discarded,
lest it lead one to regret
and lose the hope of what may be,
a potential blossom not yet set.

So gentle reader, heed my word
and nurture old and new;
For both belong in your garden
in full and lovely view.

Weed away the negative
Fertilize with love
Water strengthening roots
Look to the light above

33 THE WINDS OF CHANGE

18th October 2020

breath of history, breath of recall;
bygone innocence, unknowing all
perceptions and fancies in rose coloured hue;
life choices brim full, no limits in view

breath of the present, breath of now;
busy schedules, time races somehow
intentions and plans, these aims ever chase;
tho' worthy these causes, constraints do erase

breath of the future, breath of hope;
thoughts range wide with broader scope
wishful high lofty notions be found;
would-be horizons, reflections abound

breath of knowledge, breath of insight;
experience imparts wisdom's true light
both noble and wicked, enduring intent;
be happy and know t'was life well spent

POEM-LETS, SEASONED HAIKUS AND POINTED VERSE

In this section, the poems are short, yet are meant to be thought-provoking.

34 SILENCE

18th May 2021

they say silence is golden

but when love-worried,

silence is black granite

hard, unyielding, darkness

35 PRIDE

19th May 2021

they say it goes before a fall

but unconcealed brazen

is peacocked flagrance

self-important smugness

36 RELIEF

20th May 2021

they say it's a weight off your shoulders

but more than this,

relief is silver-tipped billows

exultant, feathery radiance

37 HOPE

21st May 2021

they say it's light at the end of a tunnel

but even more, real hope

is courageously reaching for pastel misty wisps

solidifying before one's eyes

38 FEAR

30th May 2021

they say to conquer it, you must face it

but fear is terror dread,

icy blue arctic chill,

ever shifting trepidation

39 LOVE

1st June 2021

they say all you need is love

but pink tender devotion fills not the belly

nor scarlet-worship house or clothe

ones held dear

40 SPRING-TREE

6th July 2020

Stirring young blossoms
Emerging twigs on new wood
Brownish muddy rain

41 SUMMER-TREE

5th July 2020

Sleepy slumbering
Drooping limbs laden in green
Indolent moist heat

42 AUTUMN-TREE

6th July 2020

Cascading vibrance
Windy undulating branch
Colourful curtain

43 WINTER-TREE

5th July 2020

Forest is sleeping
Giants swathed in frosty coats
Bluster in white storms

44 LOST!

25th May 2020

Lost …
I wandered past a once remembered treasure
Only to grasp smoky wisps

45 SEARCHING

25th May 2021

Searching…
    I travelled through wide horizons
Only to view changing facets of self

46 FOUND

25th May 2022

Found…
I settled, secure within familiar richness
Content to embrace firm valued truth

STORY POEMS

The next two selections are, as the title indicates, poems which tell a story. One is based on true life events and the other purely imagination.

47 THE AUDITION

For my Children
13th August 2020

The auditions were announced
They would happen in two weeks' time
I read up on the requirements:
I had the talent; I was primed
So, I sent in my application to try out for the part
Now all I needed was to prepare…
but where and how to start?
Everyone had advice for me
Everyone had something to say
Everyone had a strategy to plan for the big day

"Arrive on time!" "Be well prepared!"
"Take care to dress just right"
"Now do your best!" "Don't take a no"
"And manage your stage fright!"
I shut out all the voices though I knew
they wished me well
I needed to devise **my** scheme, **my** plan,
my own brand to sell
Checking on my schedule
Checking off the list
Checking up and making sure that
nothing else was missed

The opportunity of a lifetime!
Success here might lead to fame.
I would not waste an instant.
In a fortnight, I could make my name!
And though the date ahead loomed largely,
Fourteen days was too much to fill
How could I maintain my optimism?
There seemed too much of a stretch to kill.
Plenty of time to worry
Plenty of time to fret
Plenty of time to polish my craft;
then on the day forget!

I set myself to practicing
With energy, passion, verve
For each moment and each run through
I toiled endlessly without reserve
I honed and stretched and pulled my
skill
to lengths as yet undreamed
used every ounce of energy
as days sped by it seemed
Every day I got up early
Every day demanding more
Every day I worked hard,
grueling like I'd never done before

As the day approached closer
I did not let up my pace
Though exhausted and fatigued
I pushed towards the end of the race
Still impassioned and motivated,

I was ready to strut my stuff
But then doubts crept in uninvited,
would it all be enough?
Dry run now for the family
Dry run now for friends
Dry run now for critical peers
to clean up all loose ends

The day was finally here
I waited tensely for my turn
And as thoughts swirled round in my head
I considered what I had learned
I had executed my plan, so was ready
...both performance and mindset
Now all that remained was to share my talents;
I prayed that nothing would I forget
Would I be flawless or imperfect?
Would I be brave or full of fear?
Would I be ready? OH...they called my name, "
Oh yes...yes I am here!"

Then I suddenly realized
As I entered and took my place
And those appraising my performance
Were in their perfect viewing space
That what they were looking for didn't matter,
for today, I was the best me I could be
I would perform for this captive audience
and let all of them, see **me**!
Before the signal word was spoken
Before the signal gesture was made
Before the signal nod to start was given,

I stood tall, proud, unafraid.

For now, I really understood the plan
I took a breath....and then I began.

48 SEVEN DEADLY SINS

6th June 2020

I knocked on the door of heaven
for I hoped to get inside
The gates were gilded, golden,
and when unsealed would open wide

But as I waited to step through
for my holy home to claim
I heard voices behind me,
calling out my name

There were seven stood in the rear of me
calling out my woe
Until I faced and answered each,
forward I could not go

Their hands locked my shoulder
now I was kept in place
They smiled such evil grins at me,
and grips would not unlace

First faced I starched and haughty Pride,
with turned up nose aloft
Who spoke, "You have been in my court
not rarely but of oft
The devil rules because of me,
and invites you there to dine
For thinking that you're superior

does make you surely mine!"

And as I heard those prideful words,
my heart was steeped in shame
I recognized some selfishness
within my feeble frame
So, I tipped my cup in humility
and thus accepted my fate
But that kindness now within my heart
meant love was there, not hate

Pride's hand loosened iron grip,
gasping in dismay
Then turned to leave without a glance,
and stiffly walked away.

Next Envy in green silken suit said,
tightening up hands hold
"You've despised your neighbour's feats,
of this I have been told
You wished misfortune on your friends
so you could rise above
And smiled a fake-ness sweety smirk,
pretending you felt love"

"I have been jealous of my peers
begrudging their high goals
And I admit my lofty aims
meant raking them o'er the coals
But truly remorseful am I now
and I do wish them well
They will attain much greater heights"

this to Envy did I tell

So, Envy backed away from me,
not liking what I'd said
And now five remained holding me
in that realm of dead

"Tis I" announced a voice in back,
"Don't leave me now my, friend!"
And I saw my Sin of Gluttony,
with corpulent arm extend
Said Glutton, "You often overindulged
and others then had none
You ate and ate and didn't stop
until it all was done!"

"I wasted food, I do concede
and sometimes I wouldn't share
But there were times I know
that I gave grub to who was there
You cannot say I always gorged
and consumed far too much
Begone now please, vacate this place,
release me from your touch!"

As Gluttony portly lumbered 'way,
tighter did those left now grip
These four now there were making sure
their clutches would not slip

I knew who then addressed me
from Greed's yellow beady eye

"Your avarice meant you wanted 'Things',
it did not matter why
You hoarded, stole and kept accounts,
no portion did you allot
To those around you and especially
for those who did have not"

"I do agree for much of my life,
I ignored those in need
But before I came unto this place,
I recognized my greed
So, I donated much material wealth
to the wretched poor
I pray that they can use these gifts
and more easily endure"

Greed's eyes flashed dully at my words
and spoke of nothing more
Three left to face, three left to fear,
three left blocking the door

A silky slinky hand oozed up my back
and to my fevered brow
Lust whispered in a sultry tone
"Are the longings intense now?
For you desired, caressed the flesh,
to deny this is in vain
So come with me, and let us be
free to couple once again"

"I do admit that in my life
my thoughts have been impure

I did partake in younger years
more amply I am sure
But as I aged my wisdom grew
and gaining high regard
For the sanctity of the act,
resisting you's not hard"

Now at my words, Lust's wandering limbs
did slither from my form
Coldly rebuked now, exited,
no longer hot or warm

The sluggish intonation
from the Sin of Sloth was heard
"Both physically and mentally,
you were idle, that's the word
Disinclination to even move,
yes, you were indolent;
with nothing done, you sit
and wonder where the hours went"

"'Tis true that some laborious
occupations did I shirk
There certainly were moments
when I avoided work
But those were few,
most instances my nose was to the grind
Industrious, creative are the terms
I have in mind"

At Sloth's plodding departure,
I was close to my desire

But the one remaining, Sin of Wrath,
I greatly feared the ire
Wrath's sizzling temper, blistering rage
would burn me, this I knew
"Dare you," cried Wrath "deny your fiery nature through and through?
You've scalded souls with anger,
you've burned and stormed your friends
You've broiled and boiled and speared and seared,
means justified your ends!!"

Crestfallen wracked with guilt,
this was valid, this was real
"Wrath I beg you understand
forgiveness now is what I feel
Have patience, I am a sinner
and now soothe my thunderous heat
No more seething but pacifying,
graced forbearance is so sweet"

I tightly shut my eyes and listened
for the frenzied, cruel retort
For I knew that livid Wrath,
to deserv-ed hell me would transport

But when I dared peep to view my anguish,
I perceived bright light instead
As I marveled in awe and wonder,
comprehension reached my head
I was through the gates, in paradise,
I had knocked, was now in!

Because I had faced and answered honestly
to each and every Sin

God is mercy, God is love,
full of compassion and of care

I smiled and walked in heaven,
I was content to just...be there.

NATURE'S MIRROR

The poems in Nature's Mirror look at the natural world in all its splendour.

49 THE EVOLUTION OF RAIN

7th June 2020

Drip, drip, drip…drop!

The Infant:
Teasing source of greenery trickle
Drizzly dewy wetness tickle
Spitting, patter, napping
Tentative tiny lapping
Germinate

The Child:
Playing impish in pools and puddles
Dawdling droplets, muddy cuddles
Splashing innocent foliage flow
Plantlets sprouting; time to grow
Frolic

The Adolescent:
Cocky stormy gush cloudbursts
Torrential tempers, stamp, loud firsts!
Driving drench; no license yet
Swishing, sashaying all just wet
Maturing

The Parent:
Cleansing dirt filled earthy floor
Quenching younglings, gently pour
Patient nurture propagate

Proudly view new life create
Mother-Nature
The Senior:
Sleepy seepage
Old vines creepage
Irregular dabbling
Incoherent babbling
Dribble

All drowsy dowse…
Time for rest…

Drip, drip, drip…drop!

50 NIGHT EYES

3rd August 2020

shimmering, flickering, gleaming sparks
visible in the secret dark;
for millennia have you gazed down glowing
watching, waiting, musing, knowing.

what cryptic knowledge you've accumulated.
what novel awareness-es formulated.

you guide us from your lofty home,
when we wander, where we roam

fiery, luminous, calm, serene,
noble, radiant, pure, pristine.

silent sentinels,
bright night eyes,
ever watchful,
old and wise.

51 GENESIS OF A NEW DAY

28th April 2021

Dawn's orb peeps out at creation
beneath hooded lashes;
Still somnolent, slow stretching finger-like rays
to sky's edge:
vermillion, pale rose...
a glimmer of gold in tiny flashes
Honeyed visual melody, sweet aubade
the promise, the pledge.

Shadowy dimness evaporates
Indistinctness dissipates
Gently...now open-gaze dispels sleep-mist;
Begetting freshness, newly sun kissed

Dawn has broken; night is dispelled
Genesis of a new day, a miracle beheld

52 MOTHER NATURE'S QUIVER OF JEWELS

11th October 2020

Her flora filled quiver
spills forth a profusion
of multihued jeweled arrows

harvest-red rubies, buttery golds
warm corals, bronzed amber;
these colours she holds
tiny pearled opals and emerald greens
lush auburn garnets;
lavish riches are seen

On a sunny fall day in her Sunday best;
Her finery displayed;
Mother Nature is dressed

53 WINTERED WINGS

5th December 2020

Noble, stately heron
approaches river's edge
where snow has draped the icy wet
and blanketed the sedge

As he silently descends
and finally does alight
a graceful landing, yet disturbs
the cold and pristine white

Silent shuddering of white flakes
spills noiseless to the ground
and beneath, the carpet now more plush
snowy hillocks can be found

Feathered sovereign proudly surveys
his realm far and wide
then content, one jump, takes flight
fluid rise to flowing glide

No fanfare of his presence,
no lush royal display,
just a tiny throne of white and brown
speckled, where his feet lay

54 THUNDERFALL

26th June 2020

See out from within on a turbulent night
From the warmth of a snug, cozy room,
Stones dazzle fleetingly with flashing light
'Neath chaotic sky midst silent moon

The heavens boom with intermittent crash!
Sending echoed grumblings far and wide
While gusts bend tree limbs to snap and thrash
There is just no safe place to hide

Then comes the scouring, pelting rain
Soaking soil, leaves, rocks, flora too;
The ground now a-mud, rivulets now drain,
Erratic knocking code dispatches ensue

But within remains warm, quiet and hushed;
The dwelling a-slumber unaware
While storm rages outside, inside it's shushed;
Both in and out have donned their nightwear

55 MOUNTAINS IN THE SKY

29TH June 2020

Majestic snow-white summits fixed in the heavens
Patient…
in their anticipation

Await the climber

The one who will ascend their lofty heights
and scale them,
the peaks of billowy fog and mist,
capped in thundering shadowy darkness;
these ranges in the sky

56 FOREST BATHING

10th July 2020

meander, unhurried stroll
amidst Mother Nature's berth;
gentle raindrops, welcomed nectar
from the heavens kiss the earth

majestic timber giants
shelter tiny growing sprouts;
green leaves, brown soil, rough stalks, smooth buds
tender embrace both in and without

home to woodland creatures
varied young and aged kin;
serenely buzz, whisper, hum in chorus
in step, in tune, resonating

the path worn underfoot
densely blanketed with duff;
all residing have their place here,
belonging, cherished is enough

there is a gentle call for notice
from the floor up to the shoots;
stretch or slacken, take your ease,
feel the calming to your roots

57 GALE FORCE

28th September 2020

intense energy blows and breathes
blustering forceful power seethes
uninterrupted, unheeded straight through
reaches every instant harsh lessons it teaches

robust, venting gusts
infiltrating each corner and chink
every cleft
with intensifying windy thrusts
barreling on, huge rise, then sink
till nothing left
raze, flatten, level as everything is shaken
leaving naught as it was, all moved, all taken

its exhale grips all
spring, summer, winter, fall
never satisfied
formidable influence felt far and wide

intense energy blows and breathes
blustering forceful power seethes

58 GENTLE ZEPHYR

28th September 2020

barest breath, gentle breeze
tiptoe amidst whispering trees
meandering silks like a tangled web
moment by moment…small rise then ebb

soft caressing puff,
pervading each niche that could be,
every space
gently wafting, moving just enough
tumbling o'er land and sea…
every place
investigate, tremble, probe…lightly shake
leave rustled nothings and dustlings in its wake

its exhale touches all
spring summer, winter, fall
always gratified
feathery fingers felt far and wide

barest breath, gentle breeze
wither you float as you please

59 WALNUT TREE MEMOIR

7th October 2020

ancient gnarled wisdom
quiet, composed grace
limbs extending, protecting
comforting bough embrace

young twigs in spring
yet sturdy the bole
branched shade in hot summer
canopied beauty calms soul

cascading leaves in fall
winter blankets of snow
ever garbed in splendour
truest glory does show

gentle yet strong
heavy yet light
still yet waving
dark yet bright

lifegiving, sheltering
provides clean air for all
through decades and seasons
noble sentry stands tall

60 SNOW IN THE CHURCHYARD

5th November 2020

Powdered bone-white head and shoulders
stand cold, silent, still.
No footfall trace from man or beast
disturbs the daybreak's chill.

In that quiet peaceful dawn
row upon voiceless row,
ordered stones slumber on
beneath the virgin snow.

AND SO IT ENDS

It is often said that all good things must come to an end: good poetry, good parties, good conversations, good visits...good life.

61. THE ROAD AHEAD

We all journey down a one-way road;
No u turns, no turning back

Our carry-on luggage on our life's voyage
are stored memories, carefully packed

And as we travel, some recollections
seem to take on a lot more colour;
while others with time's passage
become more faded, duller.

We discard excess baggage
as we continue on our path;
Keeping friends and loves near;
Junking those who cause us wrath.

The speed at which we travel remains constant;
Ever forward, ever onward day by day;

But there are whiles when we feel we are hardly moving at all
as if there's a heavy toll owed we must pay.

There are also wondrous times of course,
we seem to dash at breakneck speed;
We wish we could slow ourselves down then
but life's passage does not take heed.

So, we continue advancing, ever steadfast,
reaching milestones along our route;
and we pass new attractions, new places
on our living journey commute.

We must savour the voyage, every moment;
For we'll not pass this way again.
We can't turn back the hands of time,
nor change past wheres and whens

The earth-road behind us we have traversed,
we come to realize as we age,
becomes ever, ever longer than the road ahead
before we reach the final stage…

62. BLESSING

24th January 2022

May your heart dance in the moonlight
And your laughter bubble in the sun
May the joy of just *being* fill your soul
Until the day is done

May the breezes of friendship swirl 'round you
And the dew of devotion kiss your form
May seasons of peace warm you year after year
And shelter you from every storm

May rivers of well-being flow within you
And comfort be channeled to your core
May the kindness you view in others around
Be reflected back in waves to your shore

May your heart dance in the moonlight
And your laughter bubble in the sun
May the joy of just *being* fill your soul
Until your day is done

63. BEYOND THE DOOR

27th February 2022

What lies there?

Beyond imminent horizon

What lies there?

Beyond the door

Be it pearly, luminous gate
with noble sentry in wait

Or magnificence surrounding grand vestibule;
so pure and clean, a bright sparkling jewel

Else Sovereign's royal domain
There enthroned ruler, love-powered reign

What lies there?

Beyond the distance

What lies there?

Beyond the door

Mayhap dynamic lavish hall
Where joyous delight fills one and all

No disputes or discord, surely no war
Just content kin and comrades, of recent, of yore

Perchance harped melodic chant
Jubilant exultance to each grant

What lies there?

Beyond the beyond

What lies there?

Beyond the door

64. DEATH DOESN'T CARE

13th February 2021

tick…

tock…

tick…

tock…

tomorrow I'll call or maybe the day after

I don't feel like it today

I'll mend my evil fences of hate

I'll do it, I will someday

I'll send that note to my old friend,

the one who moved afar

I'll beg forgiveness from those I've hurt

and heal that injury born scar

tick... tock… tick… tock

today I have horizons to climb

things to do, I don't have the time

maybe next week, next month, next year

for that other stuff…not now I fear

tick.tock.tick.tock
no, please...
just one more wish to make
one more breath to take
one more word to speak
one more friend to seek
just one more hello, before I go
just one last smile to share

death doesn't care

ticktock

time's up

ABOUT THE AUTHOR

LISA FREEMANTLE

Author Lisa Freemantle hails from Newmarket Ontario. Her poetry has been published in a collection by MiddleRoad Publishers called *Scaling New Heights* (2022). She is also a five-time co-author of books (Novalis Publishers) including the Words for the Journey Series, *For Teachers* and *School Liturgies Made Easy*. Besides writing poetry and prose, Lisa also composes songs and has released a number of CD's.

When she is not writing, Lisa spends most of her time directing her choir, singing, reading, walking, doing puzzles, cooking up a storm and petting the family killer cat, Smidgen.

ALSO FROM MIDDLEROAD PUBLISHERS

www.middleroadpublishers.ca

Making Literature See The Light Of Day

ALL BOOKS AVAILABLE AT AMAZON WORLDWIDE.

eBook versions available from all eBook channels

A TIME TO LOVE AN A TIME TO DIE

By Michael Joll

Finely drawn characters. Visually dramatic, tense and emotionally satisfying, this is one of the finest novels of the Great War. In this poignant story, the writing stands in stark contrast with the unvarnished brutality of trench warfare.

ATTITUDE

By Dave Moores

Fresh, gritty and laced with dry humour, Attitude is a fast-paced story readers of all ages won't want to put down. It's dead of winter and an outbreak of weird stuff, random acts of vandalism are unsettling the citizens of Southmead.

DOWN INDEPENDENCE BOULEVARD AND OTHER STORIES

by Ken Puddicombe

"A brilliant collection of stories telling the tales of people forced to leave their homes…craving the past, escaping from racial conflicts and dictatorship…"—Judith Kopacsi Gelberger, author of *Heroes Don't Cry*.

GABRIELLE

By Michael Joll

Gabrielle transcends time and space, taking the reader on a journey to Poland, France, Holland and Israel as she searches for her identity.

I WENT TO THE END OF THE RAINBOW

by Pramita Chakraborty

A beautifully illustrated, captivating tale about a young child who can't sleep and embarks on a adventure through the colours of the rainbow.

LOVE HAS TWO MOONS

By Franklin Mohan

With humour, insight and sensitivity, Franklin Mohan peels back the subtle layers of prejudice and racism in North American and Caribbean society—Raymond Holmes, author of *Witnesses and other short stories*

JUNTA

By Ken Puddicombe

"A gripping story (of) an imperfect democracy...the tension...builds increasingly from page to page."—Rico Downer, author of *There Once Was a Little England*

MEET ME AT THE FOUR CORNERS

Anthology

Twenty-six stories, fiction and non-Fiction, some of them prize winning submissions from the writers of the Brampton Writers' Guild, are featured in this collection.

PEOPLE OF GUYANA

By Ian McDonald and Peter Jailall

"These beautifully crafted poems are shaped by their generosity of spirit and abundant capacity for empathy and fun..." —Clem Seecharan

PERSONS OF INTEREST

By Michael Joll

"Exotic and intriguing! Joll brilliantly captures the reader's interest with vivid imagery and a relentless sleuth." —Phyllis Humby, short story writer, poet and novelist.

PERFECT EXECUTION AND OTHER STORIES

by Michael Joll

"Michael Joll is a master of surprise endings, but they never seem forced. He always stays true to his characters and their worlds." —Nancy Kay Clark, author and editor, *CommuterLit.com*

POEMS FOR MARY

By Ian Mc Donald

"The garden which my wife has created, it is as much a work of art as a painting by a master spirit or a piece of perfect music by a composer."—Ian Mc Donald, author, poet.

RACING WITH THE RAIN

By Ken Puddicombe

"Puddicombe's brilliant novel...an historic political conflict in Guyana, during the Cold War and the cold cynicism and tragic irony of a state sacrificed to super-power hegemony." -Frank Birbalsingh, author of *Novels and The Nation: Essays in Canadian*

RUTHLESS RHYTHMS

By Judith Gelberger

If poetry is a window into the soul of the author, Judith Gelberger has opened one which illuminates some of the most painful emotions and experiences of human existence...—Raymond Holmes - Author of *Witnesses And Other Short Stories*

SCALING NEW HEIGHTS

Anthology

Forty-two pieces from the members of Pakaraima Writers Group are featured in this their first collection of poetry and non-fiction travel articles

THE GARDEN

By Ian McDonald

Ian McDonald's poems are full of light and love. His easy style about the beauty of nature connects with his readers.

TOWARDS THE PEBBLED SHORE

By Peter Jailall

"...thoughtfully conceived, expressed movingly and written with great clarity. I think this may be Peter's best book yet. It lifts the heart."

Ian McDonald, author The Garden and other works

WEALTH THROUGH REAL ESTATE INVESTING

By Jay Brijpaul

Jay Brijpaul has tapped his vast experience and expertise in the Real Estate industry. This book provides comprehensive coverage of What, How, When, Where to invest in real estate.

UNFATHOMABLE AND OTHER POEMS

by Ken Puddicombe

These poems cover a variety of themes, all connected to a childhood growing up in British Guiana, the rise of nationalism and the pre- and post-independence eras.

WINDWARD LEGS

By Dave Moores

A pungent cocktail of choppy romance, corporate larceny and the thrills and spills of sailboat racing, Windward Legs is the rousing and captivating story of a woman's journey to rediscover who she is.

WITNESSES AND OTHER STORIES

By Raymond Holmes

"Suspenseful, historical, futuristic and riveting...stories and characters who will stay with you." —Bruce A. Hanson, Award winning author of adult and children's fiction.

www.ingramcontent.com/pod-product-compliance
Lightning Source LLC
Chambersburg PA
CBHW071311030726
47594CB00002B/392
9781990765063